Change the World for Ten Bucks

Change the World for Ten Bucks

Small Actions x Lots of People = Big Change

We Are What We Do

CHRONICLE BOOKS

SAN FRANCISCO

First published in the United States in 2009 by Chronicle Books LLC.

Copyright © 2004 by We Are What We Do CIC.
All rights reserved. No part of this book may be reproduced in any form
without written permission from the publisher.

First published in 2004 as *Change the World for a Fiver* by Short Books Ltd
in the United Kingdom.

Library of Congress Cataloging-in-Publication Data available.

ISBN: 978-0-8118-6801-3

Manufactured in China

Design by Antidote

Creative team: Tim Ashton, Steve Henry, Ken Hoggins, Chris O'Shea,
Chris Wigan, David Robinson, Eugenie Harvey, Nick Walker, Paul Twivy,
Richard Norgate, and James Chambers

Edited by Eugenie Harvey
Research by Jamie Pourier

Thanks to: Christina Amini, Kristen Hewitt, Lindsay Sablosky, J Reuben,
Morton Wagener, Emma Shaw, Tricia Sweeney, Rae Dox Kim, and Stanley Young

Cover photo by Jenna Cushner

Typeset in Clarendon BT

10 9 8 7 6 5 4 3 2 1

Chronicle Books LLC
680 Second Street
San Francisco, CA 94107
www.chroniclebooks.com

we are what we do ©

We Are What We Do is a global social change movement. We believe it is not just politicians, institutions, and big business that change the world—it is also ordinary people like you and me.

Our aim is to bring people together and demonstrate how, using simple, everyday actions, we can create a global movement of doing and changing; doing small actions and changing big problems.

We started back in 2003 with the simple question, "What would you ask one million people to do to change the world?" We received thousands of suggestions from all around the world and the result was this book, first published in the UK in 2004 and now published in countries all around the world.

But this is just the tip of the iceberg. You can find out more about us at our Web site:

www.wearewhatwedo.org

Introduction

We live in peculiar times.

More communication devices connect us than ever before, yet more people live alone. We want to belong to communities, but our cities can be very lonely places. Technology has shrunk the planet. We talk constantly on cell phones and connect online with old friends in other continents, but the time we actually spend together has decreased too. Attendance at club meetings in the United States has dropped by more than half in 25 years. Even eating together as a family has fallen by 43 percent.

Random figures perhaps, but they tell a consistent story. Most of us feel that something is now missing in our lives. We still want to make our voices heard, to feel part of something bigger than ourselves, but we no longer know how.

Maybe Mahatma Gandhi had the answer. "We must," he said, "be the change we want to see in the world." In other words, we are what we do.

So why is it so difficult?

Perhaps it is the scale of the problems which induces the state of paralysis. We think we have to leave change to governments or big business even though we also know that we elect governments and that our spending is what creates big business.

Surely the question now is not whether we should act alone, but how can we act together?

We Are What We Do is a new kind of movement—a movement with attitude. We are not trying to raise money. We are trying to show the power of a simple shift in attitudes and day-to-day behavior.

We invite you to be part of a new kind of community; not of joiners but of independent doers following the same banner and answering the questions that we all want answered.

Who are we? We Are What We Do.

How to use this book

This is a book of simple, everyday actions which we believe pretty much all of us can do. If you're reading this book, chances are you, or someone you know, has actually done one of the actions already (Action 33: Recycle Your Books or Action 47: Buy a Copy of This Book for a Friend), so you're already on the way!

A number of pages feature references to organizations that can help you perform the actions—for example, Action 26: Give Blood features the Web site address for the blood donor organization.

We've included a whole host of related Web sites in Action 49: Learn More, Do More at the end of the book, which will give you more information about the action and how to do it. We're not suggesting that either the list of actions or Web sites in Action 49 are definitive—but they are a start.

We'd love to hear from you, either with suggestions for new actions, or suggestions for other helpful organizations and Web sites. Please e-mail us at suggestions@wearewhatwedo. org and check out our Web site to see updated lists of both.

The 500 year shopping trip

Every person in the country uses an average of 330 plastic bags each year.

That's 100 billion plastic bags all together.

A plastic bag can take up to 500 years to decay in the landfill.

There is an alternative.

It's called a shopping bag; it's reusable, and apparently in France, it's very chic.

TALK TO OLD PEOPLE
THEY KNOW
COOL STUFF
YOU DON'T

Photo: Tim Ashton / Antidote

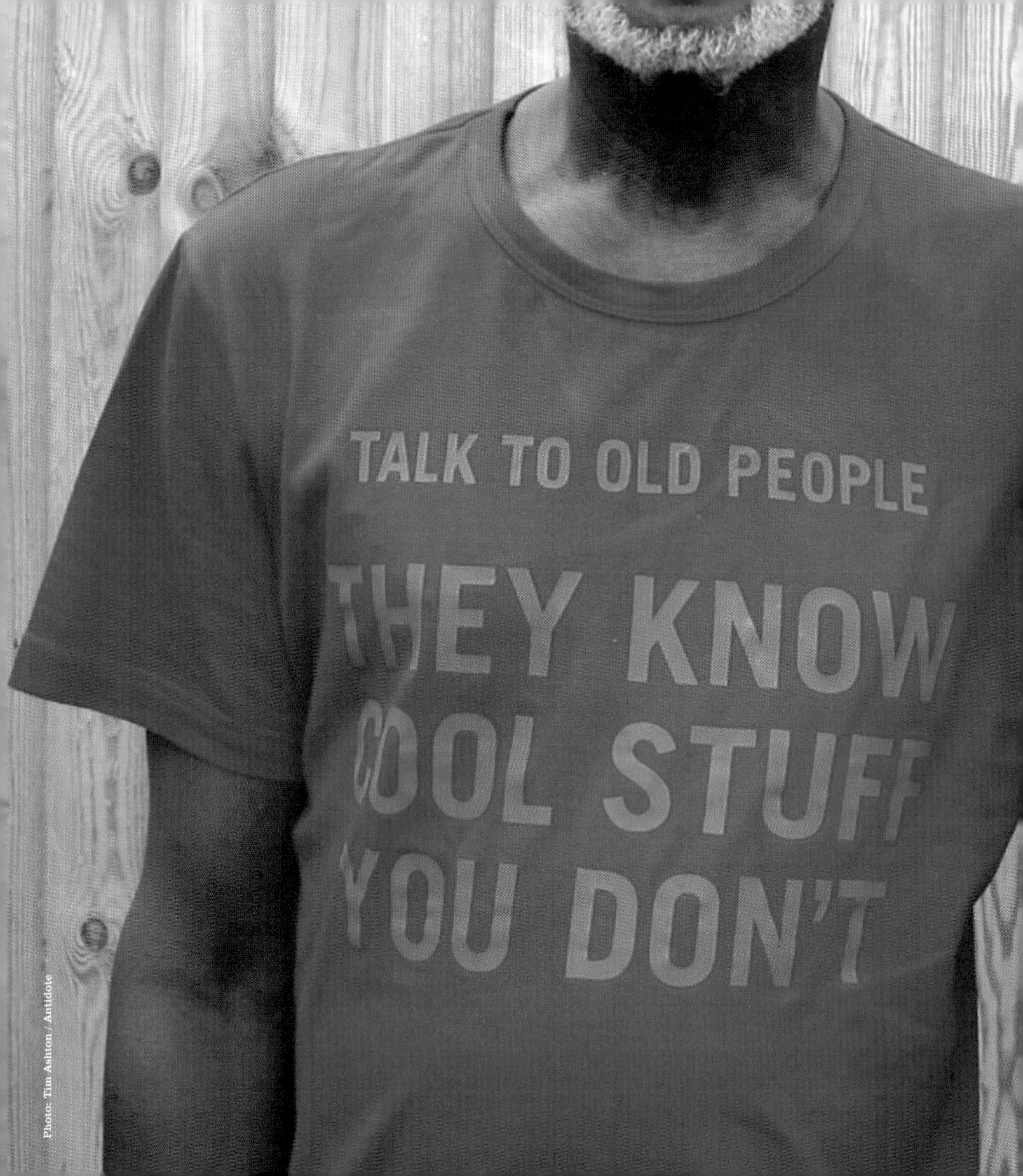

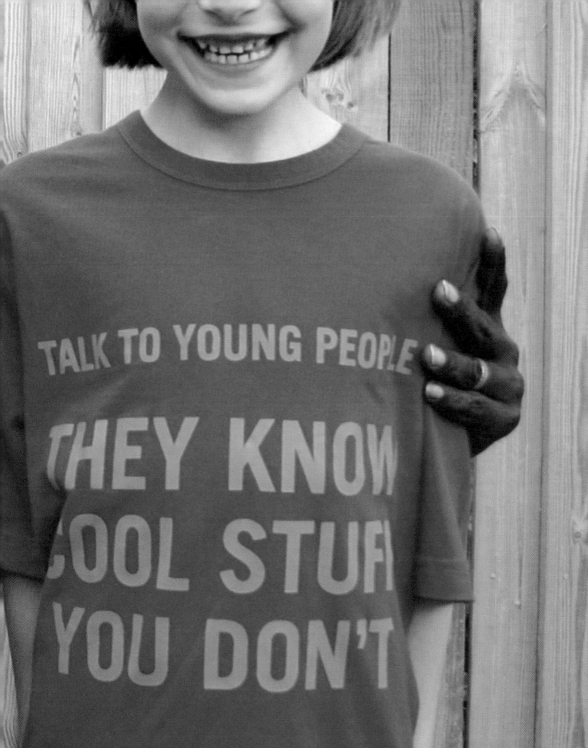

TALK TO YOUNG PEOPLE

THEY KNOW

COOL STUFF

YOU DON'T

Photo: Kevin Anthony Horgan / Getty Images

Change a lightbulb and see what you can save

An energy-saving lightbulb with an ENERGY STAR label might not seem cheap, but over its lifetime it could save you anywhere from $20–60, and a lot more besides. Like the planet for example.

Learning first aid is child's play

It only takes two hours to learn how to save a life.

What else are you going to do in that time that is going to make such a difference?

Watch American Idol twice?

And let's face it, saving someone's life is cool. In fact, it's about as cool as you can possibly get.

And, if you do learn this skill, you might like to know that the person you help is statistically unlikely to be a stranger.

They're more likely to be a friend or relative.

Imagine saving your best friend's life.

It takes half as many muscles to smile as it does to frown.

And it makes you and others feel twice as good.

A bus carries the same number of people as 20 cars.
And it's going there anyway.

Go play in the dirt

After all those years of your mother telling you not to, we're making an appeal to the rebel in you.

Flowers, vegetables, herbs, house plants, bamboo, ferns, trees—we don't mind what it is, just get planting.

You'll turn carbon dioxide into oxygen, calm your mind, relax your body, and potentially have something delicious to eat.

Even being short on space is an opportunity to get creative and connect with your inner child by planting bean sprouts in an egg shell.

Save water. Have fun. Just get out before everything becomes wrinkled.

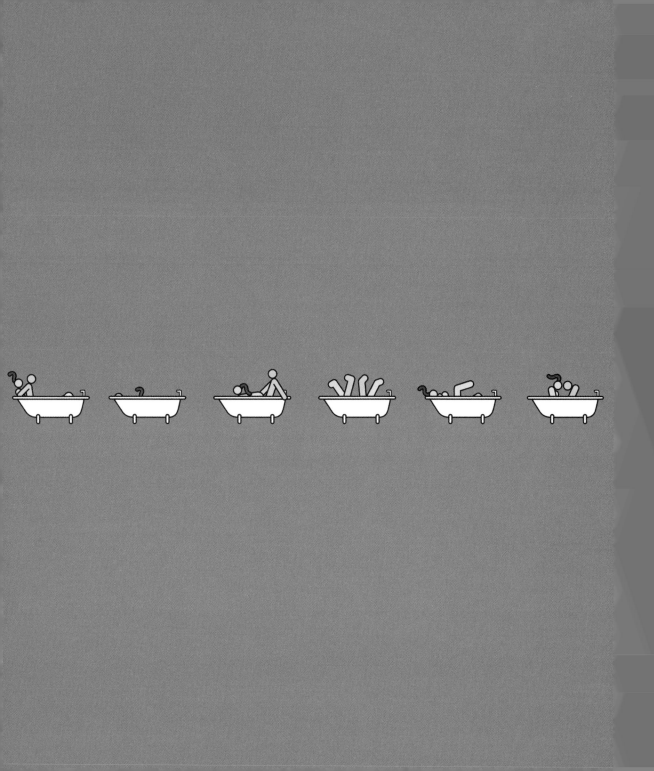

We're
OPEN

Come on in and have a look around. How are you today?
We've got some of those cookies you said you liked.
They're turning out to be quite a popular choice down the street.
Oh, don't worry if you haven't got enough change on you, just
give it to me next time you're in.

See you tomorrow.

We're

CLOSED

So sorry, hope you don't need anything too urgent.
The thing is, not enough of you have been coming to see us recently. We think it might have something to do with the big shop that's opened up down the road.
We've loved being here but just can't afford to stay open any more.

See you.

Solar power

Mother Nature's clothes dryer is proof that sometimes the original is still the best.

As you hang your pants in the breeze, remember that just one load of laundry in the dryer uses enough energy to make 250 pieces of toast—a savings of up to $100 a year.

Use a clothesline or a foldable drying rack and start hanging to take advantage of the world's oldest, free clothes dryer.

Walk more

Obesity is a massive problem in the United States. According to the Center for Disease Control and Prevention, in 2007 Colorado was the only state with an obesity rate under 20 percent.

Three states were over 30 percent, but let's not point fingers.

One suggestion from doctors is to do something simple such as walking up a couple flights of stairs every day.

Or try walking as much as you can.

Even if it's only to the corner store.

Math will be on your side to burn some of those calories.

A TV that's plugged in is still using half the electricity of a TV that's turned on

Most appliances—VCRs, DVD players, televisions, stereos, computers, and kitchen appliances—use power even when they are switched off.

For the average home, 75 percent of the electricity used to power home appliances is used while the products are not in use and turned off.

It's still costing you money and wasting energy.

Do the planet, and yourself, some good by unplugging appliances or using a power strip with a switch to shut off the flow of electricity.

There are 130 million cell phones thrown away in the United States every year. That's a hell of a lot of annoying ringtones, and worse, it equates to 65,000 tons of landfill waste.

That's about the same as burying 43 World War II destroyers. And that's not even counting the millions of old cell phones lying around in people's desk drawers.

So, despite the strong desire to grab the Flip Up 2200 from the guy next to you in line and chuck it in the garbage can, resist.

The least irritating thing about your cell phone should be how it is used after its death.

Go to http://recyclemycellphone.org to send in your phone for recycling, or check out http://earth911.org and enter your zip code to find a recycling drop off point near you.

When kids ask you to read a story to them, it's because they know something you don't.
They know you'll both feel richer for the experience.

REGISTER AS
A DONOR
ONLINE

After you've died, let your heart beat inside someone else's chest.

Let your liver live, after you've passed on.

Even your eyes could give someone else a new look.

Many of us support organ donation in principle, but the truth is 17 people die each day waiting for a transplant due to the shortage of registered donors.

To make sure your wishes are carried out, you need to do two things:

First, tell your next of kin about your wishes. Otherwise, in the heat of their distress, they might rescind your decision.

Second, go to www.organdonor.gov/donor to find out what you need to do to register as an organ donor in your state.

Lose money instantly

There's always loose change—and there are
always charity donation tins.

It's a match made in heaven—like bacon and
eggs, Batman and Robin, or Paris Hilton
and . . . well Paris Hilton and the paparazzi.

If we all put our spare change into charity
donation tins, the world would be a lot
better off.

So, the next time you buy something and
get change back, look around for the
donation tin.

After all, one cent per person per week adds
up to $156 million per year.

Rearrange your pictures.

Make a cocktail.

File.

Write a song.

Apply makeup.

Swim in a pond.

Wear gold.

Revert to childhood.

Stay up all night.

Change your hair color.

Turn left instead of right.

Streak.

Massage someone.

Dust.

Shave something off.

	Arabic	Chinese	Polish
Hello	Salaamu Alaikum (Peace Be Upon You)	Nee How	Czesc
Good-bye	Salaamu Alaikum (Peace Be Upon You)	Jie Jian	Do widzenia
Please	Min Fadluk	Ching	Prosze
Thank you	Shukran	Se Se	Dziekuje
Can I help?	Ma yumkin an as 'ad?	Wo leng bung joma?	Czy moge pomoc?
Would you like a cup of tea?	Sawfa anta/anti minal fanjan shai?	Ni yow bu yow yi bay cha?	Czy napijesz sie herbaty?

Bengali	Tamil
Assalam mu alaikum	Vanakam
Khuda hafeez	Santhipoum
Doya kore	Thayavu
Doyno baad	Nintri
Shajoy korte pari?	Uthavi saiyava?
Aponi ki cha pan korben?	Unkalku thenri thartuma?

Ma yumkin an as 'ad?

Yes, you can help actually.

Just by learning a few words in a foreign language, it's amazing how much genuine warmth you can generate.

It's not something we tend to do, but it's a lot easier than you think.

For instance, in Italian the word for "hello" is the same as the word for "good-bye."

Which is a lovely sentiment, although it could make telephone calls rather confusing.

'...So the dog said...'

Make people laugh at you

Learn at least one good joke.

Laughing tones your stomach, lowers your blood pressure, and makes you healthier. It's scientifically proven.

Even the concentration of salivary immunoglobulin A is raised by laughing—and this guards our respiratory tract from infectious organisms.

But that in itself isn't very funny. Unlike the one about the two certain things in life being death and taxes. Oh wait, that isn't funny either, just true.

Make sure your investments have the same values as you

Unless you check that your retirement fund is ethically invested, chances are you're supporting the arms industry and companies with poor human and environmental records.

Now, this is a complicated area, and even if you're just thinking about your retirement fund, you deserve some kind of medal.

So, to make this as simple as possible—just ask your retirement provider one question: "Can you ensure that my investments don't harm the planet or hurt my fellow man?"

If we all did that, retirement providers would soon take notice.

But don't get caught up in a longer conversation, unless you're desperate for company.

As Woody Allen once said, anybody who wants to know the definition of eternity should try spending an evening talking to a life insurance salesman.

The most beautiful view of Manhattan

All those offices with lights burning bright at night.

Are they really all full of people working late?

Or is it some cock-eyed theory of aesthetics which says that lighting an empty space is beautiful?

Ivory was considered beautiful once.

Fur was considered beautiful once.

In 2007,
Nina Wang
left her
$4 billion
fortune
to her
fortune teller,
Tony Chan.

In 1926, Charles Vance Millar,
a wealthy Toronto lawyer,
bequeathed his estate
to whichever woman gave birth
to the most babies in the
ten-year period
following his death.

Robert Miller,
who passed away in 1995,
did his part to reduce
the annoying traffic situations
caused by double-parking
by bequeathing $5,000
as reward money
for officers who write
the most tickets
for double-parking.

Have the will to make a will

Even a basic will is better than nothing at all.

You can go to an office supply or software store and purchase one of the various How to Make a Will type software packages, or even a do-it-yourself book will aid you in making a legally binding will.

In 1946, prospector James Kidd gave his estate to research to find scientific proof that a soul leaves the human body at death.

Housewife Mary Kuhery is reported to have left her husband $2 as long as he promised to spend at least half of it on a rope with which to hang himself.

Mark Gruenwald, Marvel Comics writer, left instructions in his will for his ashes to be combined with ink and then have the mixture used within the pages of a comic book in 1996.

Audrey Jean Knauer left $290,000 to the actor Charles Bronson whom she adored.

Wham-O frisbee designer Ed Headrick's dying wish was for his ashes to be molded into memorial discs, and the profits of the sales go to a museum dedicated to the frisbee.

THE PLEASURE OF THE
COMPANY OF

Our family

IS REQUESTED TONIGHT
AT THE KITCHEN TABLE

TO

GET TOGETHER FOR
A FAMILY MEAL

BRING
CONVERSATION

Research has shown that children who have meals
with their parents are much less likely to suffer from
anxiety or stress disorders.

So why not try chatting to each other?

George H. Bush said that America needed more families
like the Waltons, and less like the Simpsons.

A very bad idea, as it happens—after all, when
was the last time you laughed at the Waltons?

But if you notice, even the Simpsons like to eat together.

Here's something
to chew on

Americans chew an average of 300 pieces of gum—which isn't biodegradable yet—every year.

Where do these 1 1/2 pounds of chewed-up gum each person produces go?

On the sidewalk? On the street? Under the table?

Shame, shame, shame.

Next time you're done savoring your favorite flavor, put it in the trash instead. If everyone did that, we wouldn't waste any more time cursing when we step in gum.

Because there wouldn't be any to step in.

Every year Americans throw away an estimated
25 billion Styrofoam cups, which is enough to
circle Earth about 400 times.

Additionally, 410,000 paper cups are used every 15
minutes in the United States for hot beverages.

Where? Where do they all come from? Is there some
mad genius breeding them in underground bunkers?
Do they sneak out at night and eat our leftovers?

I could have sworn I just saw two of them
whispering to each other in the garbage can.

But why not just put your coffee into a mug,
not a Styrofoam or paper cup? It'll taste better,
and you'll be doing your part for the planet.

www.givelife.org

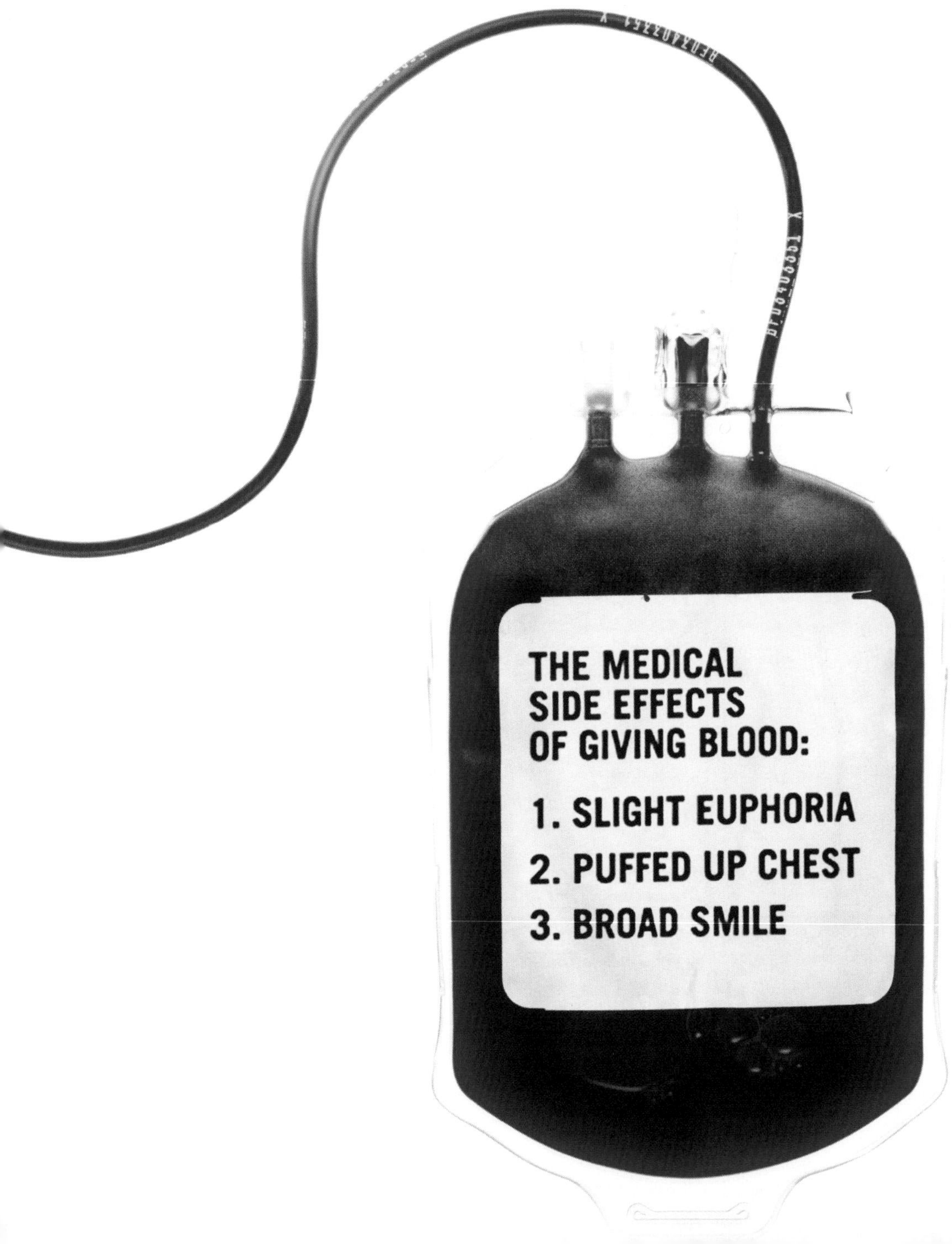
THE MEDICAL
SIDE EFFECTS
OF GIVING BLOOD:
1. SLIGHT EUPHORIA
2. PUFFED UP CHEST
3. BROAD SMILE

The art of reverse haggling

Confuse the wonderful people who work in thrift stores.
Pay them more than they bargained for.

"We must be the change we want to see in the world."

—Mahatma Gandhi

Document - Microsoft Word

File　Edit　View　Insert　Format　**Tools**　Table　Window　Help

Chuck　▶

Leave on street　▶

Throw in attic　▶

Take to dump　▶

Donate to local school

Page 1　Sec 1　1/1　At 2.5cm　Ln 1　Col 1　REC　TR

What we say about glasses in Action 42 applies equally to computers. Except that computers are slightly heavier to carry around.

So, if you've got a computer you don't need anymore, contact any of the Web sites mentioned in Action 49, and they'll help you get it to someone who can make good use of it.

Imagine the joy a seven-year-old would feel if he could play with the mightiest thing ever invented. The thing you currently use to play Minesweeper and visit dating sites.

OVR

Ready, set, give

Next time you need to buy a friend a
present, don't. Make them one instead.

Gingerbread Men

1/2 cup softened butter

1/2 cup sugar

1 egg, lightly beaten

2 tablespoons light corn syrup

2 cups plain flour

2 teaspoons baking soda

1/4 teaspoon salt

1 teaspoon cinnamon

1 teaspoon ground ginger

Preheat oven to 350°F.

Cream together butter and sugar.

Beat in the egg and syrup.

Sift in the dry ingredients and mix.

Chill the dough before rolling onto a lightly
floured board, to a 1/8 inch thickness.

Cut into shapes, using a gingerbread cutter.

Bake on a lightly greased tray for 8–10 minutes.

Give away immediately.

Save the world while brushing your teeth

Most people leave the faucet running while brushing their teeth.

This wastes more than 2 gallons a minute!

This means your street alone could fill an Olympic sized swimming pool each year.

This wastes huge amounts of water and is a bit stupid—it's like having the toilet flush the whole time you're on it.

So why not turn off the faucet while you brush your teeth?

(We bet this is one of the actions you don't forget from this book. For some reason, it seems to strike a chord with everyone.)

Who says you can't draw?

Ever wondered why Bob Ross always looked so cheerful and had such a chilled out voice?

Nobody really knows. But maybe it's because he knew the therapeutic effects of art.

It's fun to draw—and surprisingly easy.

Get a pencil and paper and copy the picture opposite as it is (upside down). Then turn your picture right side up and, chances are, you've drawn a much better picture than you've ever drawn before.

And you'll find that you've confronted and defeated a prejudice you had about yourself.

Then, if you're inspired, go to our Web site and pick up more tips on how to do things you've never done before.

Give away some great ideas

They dreamed up a scheme in Amsterdam a few years ago, where white bicycles were provided free. And the idea was that—after you'd finished your ride—you'd leave the bike in the street for someone else to use free.

And if that isn't recycling, we don't know what is.

But unfortunately this idea flopped, because they failed to take into account two things:

One, the fact that criminals exist. And two, the fact that colored paint exists.

But the idea was fantastically optimistic and deserved to succeed.

A better version of this might be to ask people to recycle their books. Give them to a thrift store, your local library, or just leave them lying on a park bench.

Happiness is a fair-trade banana

Fair-trade products guarantee to give the people who grow them a fair share of the profits. You'll see all sorts of fair-trade products in the stores these days—from bananas to coffee. So, if you buy a fair-trade banana, you can be proud of your banana.

And there are few feelings in this world that are better than being proud of your banana.

Nice to do. Nice to get. What is there not to like about it?

Don't just do something.
Sit there.

In the United States alone, 118 million prescriptions were for antidepressants in 2005. How big has that number grown since?

Depression affects a huge number of people. But there are lots of little things we can all do to make the world a less depressing place.

Like . . . just listening.

It's a real art, actually—and not as easy as it sounds.

Listen to someone, don't make any comments, don't try to solve their problems.

Just listen.

Beat road rage

At least 1,500 people are injured or killed each year due to road rage in the United States.

Here's an idea. The next time you're at an intersection, let a car out ahead of you—but only if it's less cool than your own car.

If we all did that, the world would be a better place.

And if someone driving a Ford Pinto lets you out first, don't worry about it.

It's not personal.

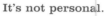

After you!

Only fill the kettle with the water you need

Save time, energy, and H_2O by making your next cup of oolong or Darjeeling tea with an electric tea kettle.

An old school stove-top tea kettle will take about nine minutes to boil a mere four cups of water.

Its electric counterpart will take under five.

The Brits use these little electric wonders and let's face it, they know their tea.

It also makes a great cup of hot chocolate, all in the amount of time it takes you to find the marshmallows in the cupboard.

Your cell phone charger is more powerful than it looks. And 95 percent of the energy used by phone chargers is wasted. They're only doing their job—charging phones—for 5 percent of the time.

350.org
nationalparksociety.com
knitting.meetup.com
thendl.com
us.mensa.org
amnesty.org
piecouncil.org
usairguitar.com
greenpeace.org
elvisinsiders.com
ncpc.org
peacecorps.gov
ajli.org
isurfing.com
pewtrusts.org
wineappreciation.com
nmai.si.edu
gocampingamerica.com
poetrysociety.org
juggling.org
pbs.org
nationalgeographic.com
fedflyfishers.org
coopamerica.org
broadwayacrossamerica.com
constitutionparty.com
democrats.org
gp.org
lp.org
rnc.org
aspca.org
harley-davidson.com
girlscouts.org
scouting.org
ffa.org
npr.org
metmuseum.org
barefooters.org
spellingbee.com
spymuseum.org
epicurious.com
volunteermatch.org
sierraclub.org
readinggroupchoices.com
si.edu
dennysbeerbarrelpub.com
newyork.fgi.org
garden.org
astronomy.com
usclubsoccer.org
lasvegasfanclub.com

Long gone are the days when joining
something meant bringing a dish for
the potluck or helping to raise the barn.

These days, joining in can simply mean
logging on. Who knows, you might just
be inspired to get off the couch too.

A friend of mine has never
forgotten seeing his father
kiss his grandpa's hand as
he lay in a coma, just before
he died.

It was the only time he had
ever seen them kiss.

And the only time he hugged
his father was when his
sister died.

It wasn't that they weren't
close, just that they were
grown up, they were men,
and American, and only
death could take down all
the barriers.

But children do it
instinctively—they
want to touch and
be touched, to hold
and be held.

So if there was one
bit of advice we'd give
everyone reading this
book, it would be this:

Touch someone you love.

Hold them.

Stroke them.

Kiss them.

It's the one piece of magic
we can all do, every day.

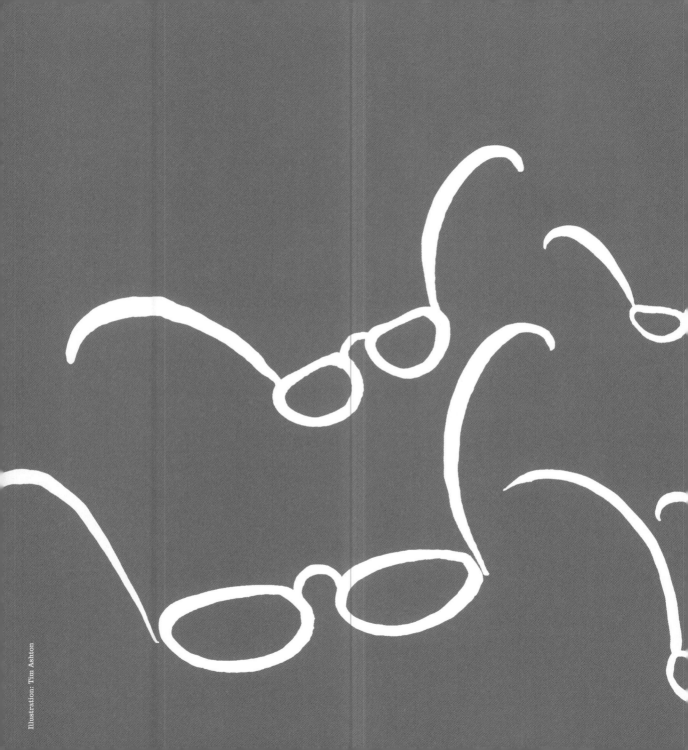

Every year thousands of pairs of specs could be flown to developing countries

Many of us have old pairs of glasses lying around unused.

Yet over 153 million people around the world need glasses every year.

People who can't see properly can't do their jobs, and kids who can't see properly can't learn at school.

So don't chuck out your old specs, check out recycling programs.

One such program is the Lions Recycle for Sight.

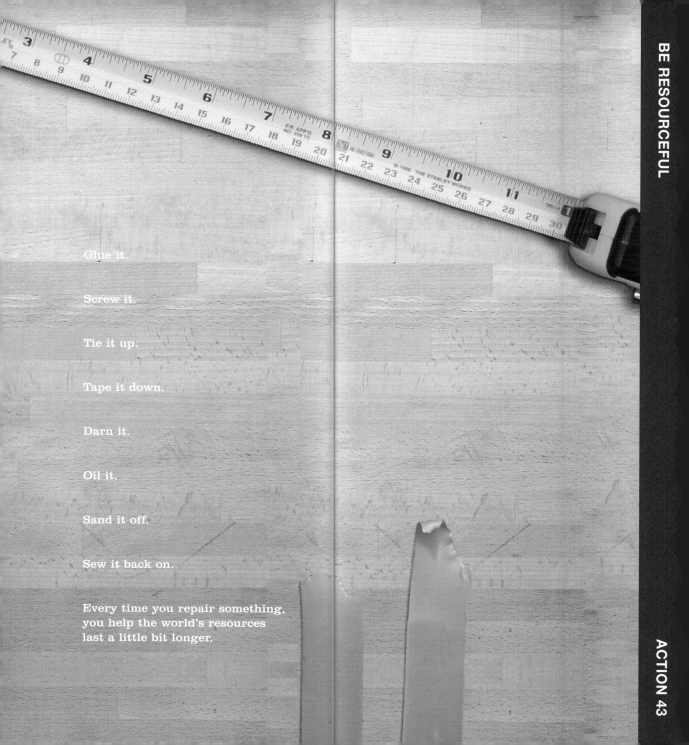

Glue it.

Screw it.

Tie it up.

Tape it down.

Darn it.

Oil it.

Sand it off.

Sew it back on.

Every time you repair something,
you help the world's resources
last a little bit longer.

Spot the difference

Turning down your thermostat when you leave home for work or play, can save you money and energy.

If it's too challenging to do this on your own, invest in a programmable thermostat.

It does the legwork for you and can save you up to two hundred bucks a year in heating costs.

Talk to strangers.
Start next door.

Give your phone number
to five people on your street.

Why not?

They could help you, you
could help them, you could
make new friends.

My name is: _____

I'm your neighbor.

My phone number is: _____

Please call if I can help.

My name is: _____

I'm your neighbor.

My phone number is: _____

Please call if I can help.

My name is: _____

I'm your neighbor.

My phone number is: _____

Please call if I can help.

My name is: _____

I'm your neighbor.

My phone number is: _____

Please call if I can help.

My name is: _____

I'm your neighbor.

My phone number is: _____

Please call if I can help.

we are what we do©

we are what we do©

we are what we do©

we are what we do©

we are what we do©

Use of every paper

93 percent of all U.S. office waste by weight is paper.

So much for the so-called paperless office that everyone was writing staff memos about a few years back.

But if we used both sides of the sheet—for instance by pressing the button that says "use both sides of the paper" on the photocopier—we could halve this.

Let's create a culture in which we make it socially unacceptable to use only one side of paper.

both

sides

piece

of

THIS BOOK
BELONGS TO

Isn't this a little bit self-serving, an advertisment for our book at the end of our book?

But this isn't about making money, it's about making change.

For change to really happen, at least a million people have to adopt the actions in this book.

So, after you've bought your copy, buy another.

And then give it to the person you think needs it most.

You know the one.

What would you like one million people to do?

One man or woman can change the way we act every day. One such man was Martin Luther King, Jr.

Send us your ideas for what you'd like one million people to do, and we'll make them part of the We Are What We Do movement.

suggestions@wearewhatwedo.org

The 50 simple actions in this book are just a beginning. Here are some Web sites to give you more ideas and inspiration.

01	DECLINE PLASTIC BAGS WHENEVER POSSIBLE	www.plasticbagrecycling.org
		www.reusablebags.com
02	SPEND TIME WITH SOMEONE OF A DIFFERENT GENERATION	www.globalaging.org
		http://seniorjournal.com/Volunteers.htm
03	SWITCH TO AT LEAST ONE ENERGY-SAVING LIGHTBULB	www.edf.org
04	LEARN BASIC FIRST AID	www.redcross.org
05	SMILE AND SMILE BACK	www.cuteoverload.com
06	TAKE PUBLIC TRANSPORT WHEN YOU CAN	www.publictransportation.org
		www.coolcalifornia.org
07	PLANT SOMETHING	www.communitygarden.org
08	HAVE A BATH WITH SOMEONE YOU LOVE	www.wateruseitwisely.com
09	SHOP LOCALLY	http://staylocal.org/info/why
		www.shoplocal.com
10	HANG YOUR WASHING OUT TO DRY	www.laundrylist.org
11	GET MORE FIT AND FEEL BETTER	www.walkinginfo.org
12	UNPLUG APPLIANCES WHEN NOT IN USE	www.eere.energy.gov
13	RECYCLE YOUR CELL PHONE	http://earth911.org
14	READ A STORY WITH A CHILD	www.readingrockets.org
15	REGISTER ONLINE AS AN ORGAN DONOR	www.organdonor.gov
16	GIVE YOUR CHANGE TO CHARITY	www.unicefusa.org
17	TRY WATCHING LESS TV	http://kidshealth.org
18	LEARN TO BE FRIENDLY IN ANOTHER LANGUAGE	http://translate.google.com
19	LEARN ONE GOOD JOKE	www.getamused.com
20	FIND OUT HOW YOUR MONEY IS INVESTED	www.maketiaa-crefethical.org
21	TURN OFF UNNECESSARY LIGHTS	www.earthhour.org
22	USE YOUR WILL TO GOOD EFFECT	http://www.nolo.com
23	HAVE MORE MEALS TOGETHER	www.everydayfoodmag.com
24	PUT YOUR GUM IN THE TRASH	http://www.treehugger.com
25	USE A MUG NOT A DISPOSABLE CUP	http://mugs.cafepress.com
26	GIVE BLOOD	www.givelife.org
27	PAY MORE WHEN YOU BUY AT THRIFT STORES	http://thethriftshopper.com/
28	SEIZE THE MOMENT	www.stanford.edu/group/king
		www.mkgandhi.org
29	RECYCLE YOUR COMPUTER	www.epa.gov/e-cycling/donate.htm
		http://sharetechnology.org/
30	BAKE SOMETHING FOR A FRIEND	www.epicurious.com
31	TURN OFF THE FAUCET WHILE BRUSHING YOUR TEETH	www.usagreen.org/waterConservation.html
32	DO SOMETHING YOU THINK YOU CAN'T DO	www.bobross.com
		www.worldwidelearn.com
33	RECYCLE YOUR BOOKS	www.ala.org

We Are What We Do does not receive money from any Web sites mentioned in this book and is not responsible for their content.

Practice active listening with friends, coworkers, and family

Tell those you love, especially the children in your life, how special they are

Go to a farmers' market

Send a real, honest-to-goodness letter in the mail to an old friend

Group errands together to save gas

Switch to reusable bottles instead of plastic ones

Keep a promise

Pick an organization you believe in and donate to it every month

Host a happy hour get-together for friends at your home

Reuse plastic baggies for sandwiches

Respect one another

Share your umbrella

Drop a dollar and don't pick it up

Paint with your kids

Write to elected officials

Befriend a person of a different political party

Speak with a different generation around a family meal table

Bring back manners

Live each day as if it were your last

Support local and independent businesses

Read a national newspaper

Hang up your hunting rifle

Love unconditionally

Stop littering

Write a love note on

Think of others first

your sidewalk in chalk

Count your blessings

Drive as if you know everyone

Take part in a carpool

in town personally

If you have to say "have a nice day," try to mean it

Smile more and complain less

Write a letter to the editor of your local paper

Stop and smell the roses

Give to charities at holidays/birthdays in the name of your friends/relatives

Say hi to someone you don't know

Pick up trash and dispose of it properly

Learn something new

Do one selfless act for someone else

Start a community garden

Grow a vegetable

Invite new acquaintances over for a meal

Sit on your porch more often and talk with neighbors

Trade unused clothes and sporting equipment

Limit shower time

Create a neighborhood lending library

Love yourself

Stop watering your lawn—and pavement

Join the 350 movement

Start up a weekly game of Ultimate Frisbee in your neighborhood greenspace

Buy a can of

Take a neighbor's dog for a walk

food to donate

Switch cleaning products for green products **Cook dinner for someone and don't let them help clean up**

Teach a young person how to can food

Laugh at yourself—soon and often

Be a mentor

Don't idle your car when parked

Keep your tires inflated

Hold a block party Compost

Deliver flowers to a nursing home or hospice

One day a year, go without electronic appliances

Use recycled water to water outdoor plants

Do more yoga

Don't drive and talk on your cell phone

Run an errand for an elderly neighbor or single parent

Take a self-defense class

Turn your air conditioning off one night a week

Recycle as much as possible

Recycle disposable plastic glasses

Turn off the Game Boy and talk to an older person

Vote

Brown bag your lunch, or better yet, use a reusable bag daily

Put yourself in someone else's shoes

Put a pot of flowers on your front steps

Simplify your life

Give more than you take

Open the door for others

Ride your bike

Deliver homemade pies to your friends and neighbors

Don't park in a handicap zone if you are not handicapped

Hand a cool drink or coffee to the crossing guard

Throw a slow-food dinner party

Buy a glass of lemonade from a lemonade stand

Use glass instead of plastic cups

Don't buy a hot tub

Ask for a young person's help

Ask everyone to go veg for a few days a week

Plant a butterfly garden

Buy something used

Mentor a refugee

Find a body of water and put your feet in it

Leave a big tip

Reuse those gift bags you get gifts in

Adopt a shelter pet instead of going to a breeder

Sing out loud

Thank you for all your fabulous suggestions for new actions. Please keep sending them to us and get more great ideas from www.wearewhatwedo.org.

we are what we do©